A SENSE OF LIFE IN The Sixties

R. G. Grant

This edition published in 2000 by
Wayland Publishers Ltd.

First published in 1999 by
Wayland Publishers Ltd,
61 Western Road,
Hove,
East Sussex BN3 1JD

Copyright © Wayland Publishers Ltd, 1999

This book was prepared for Wayland Publishers Ltd
by Ruth Nason.

Series editor: Alex Woolf
Series design: Stonecastle Graphics/Carole Design
Book design: Ruth Nason

Find Wayland on the internet at:
http://www.wayland.co.uk

British Library Cataloguing in Publication Data

Grant, R. G.
    A look at life in the sixties
    1.History, Modern - 20th century - Juvenile
    literature
    2.Nineteen sixties - Juvenile literature
    I.Title II.Sixties
    909.8'26

ISBN 0 7502 2655 2

Printed and bound in Italy by G. Canale & C.S.p.A.,
Turin

Cover photographs

Top left: West Berliners wave across the
Berlin Wall, 1961 (Popperfoto)

Top right: The Beatles, 1963 (Popperfoto)

Centre: Leonard Nimoy as Mr Spock
in *Star Trek* (Paramount Television,
courtesy Kobal)

Bottom left: Hippies at a 'happening',
selling beads, bells and badges, in
London (Topham Picturepoint)

Bottom right: Astronaut 'Buzz' Aldrin
on the Moon, July 1969, with the
reflection of Neil Armstrong in his
helmet (Popperfoto)

Acknowledgements

The Author and Publishers thank the following for
their permission to reproduce photographs: Anglo
Enterprise/Vineyard (courtesy Kobal): page 39t;
Camera Press: pages 10, 12t, 16b, 18b, 19, 22tr,
22b, 29b, 41b; Hulton Getty: pages 5, 6b, 7b, 9,
11b, 12b, 13t, 17, 18t, 20r, 23, 30t; Kobal
Collection: page 38b; Popperfoto: pages 4b, 6t, 7t,
8t, 8b, 11t, 13b, 14b, 21t, 21br, 22tl, 25, 26t, 31,
32t, 32b, 33, 34t, 35t, 35b, 37t; Retna Pictures:
pages 24t, 24b, 26b, 27b, 37b; Topham Picturepoint: pages 4t, 14t, 15t, 16t, 20l, 21bl, 27t, 28b,
29t, 30b, 36, 40, 41t; 20th Century Fox (courtesy
Kobal): pages 38t, 39b.

Contents

A Look at...

...in the '60s

A LOOK AT
THE NEWS
IN THE '60s

▽ *Hippies at a pop festival in the late 1960s.*

A famous song of the 1960s, by Bob Dylan, was 'The times they are a-changing'. There was a feeling of optimism, a sense that life could be changed for the better. In Western Europe and North America at least, people were better-off than ever before. There were jobs for all, and every year there were more consumer goods that ordinary families could afford to buy. But the decade was also a time of bitter social conflicts and brutal warfare.

Young people and the 'generation gap'

Society was full of young people. A high birth rate in the late 1940s and early 1950s meant that schools and universities were expanding. With more money in their pockets, young people had more independence. Many rejected the hard-working, conservative way in which their parents had lived. They wanted more fun. The 'generation gap' between teenagers and their parents was endlessly debated.

Hippies

In the mid-1960s the Hippie movement grew up in the Haight Ashbury district of San Francisco.

Profile

Che Guevara

Many students in the later 1960s had a poster of Argentinian-born revolutionary Ernesto 'Che' Guevara on their wall. He was the right-hand man of Fidel Castro, who had carried out a successful revolution in Cuba in 1959. In 1965 Guevara left Cuba to spark revolutions around the world. He tried to start an uprising in Bolivia and was killed there in 1967.

Che's example appealed to young people who had a romantic view of the need for a revolution to change the world for the better.

...Newsflash...

Monterey, June 1967. Since the start of this year, the children of white middle-class families have been tuning in to Flower Power. At mass open-air festivals, beginning with a 'Be-In' in San Francisco, thousands have been introduced to the chanting of mantras and smoking marijuana. Now they are calling this the 'Summer of Love' as young people with flowers in their hair flock to music events like the International Pop Festival at Monterey.

Hippies wanted to create an ideal world based on peace and love, in which there would be no money and no work. Few people tried to live a full Hippie lifestyle, but many were influenced by their 'flower power' attitudes.

Young people and politics

Some young people, especially students, became involved in political protest. Many students felt that the older generation had ruined the world with wars, racism, pollution and a joyless lifestyle. Some decided that the answer was a revolution in the way society was run. In 1968, France was brought to a standstill by a student uprising, and there was major disruption also in Germany, Italy and the USA.

A young man involved in revolutionary politics in London in the 1960s, Horace Ove talked later about what he had felt a revolution would bring:

'Maybe racism would come to an end in every racist country, wars ... would come to an end, and we would see a more loving, understanding, communicating world ...'

▷ *Riot police charge student demonstrators in Paris, June 1968. All the student revolts failed in the face of tough action by the authorities.*

△ *Soviet tanks in Prague, Czechoslovakia, in August 1968.*

In Northern Ireland, students took the lead in protests in favour of equal rights for Catholics. The movement met with a violent reaction from Protestants and this led to British troops being sent on to the streets in 1969.

Young people were in the forefront of the 'Prague Spring' of 1968, when communist Czechoslovakia was swept by a movement for liberal reform. However, the reform movement was soon crushed. Troops from the Soviet Union and its allies invaded Czechoslovakia and restored the old communist order.

Even in communist China, in 1966 the dictator Mao Tse-tung encouraged young people, the Red Guards, to attack teachers and other authority figures in what was called the Cultural Revolution.

The Cold War

The USA and its allies confronted the communist Soviet Union and its allies in the Cold War. Both sides had nuclear weapons ready for delivery against one another's cities at a minute's notice. In the early 1960s both sides carried out nuclear tests, exploding devices that scattered nuclear fallout into the atmosphere.

The USA and the Soviet Union ran large espionage organizations, the CIA and the KGB, which often grabbed the headlines. In 1960 a US U2 spy plane was shot down over the Soviet Union and its pilot, Gary Powers, was captured. In 1963, a spy scandal rocked British politics when it turned out that the defence minister, John Profumo, had been sharing a girlfriend with a Soviet spy.

▷ *Red Guards in Peking carry images of Mao Tse-tung, August 1966.*

The Iron Curtain and the Berlin Wall

An 'Iron Curtain' was said to divide the communist countries of Eastern Europe from democratic Western Europe. Behind the Iron Curtain, the German city of Berlin was jointly controlled by NATO countries (Britain, France and the USA) and the Soviet Union.

In 1961 the Soviets and their East German allies built a wall across the centre of Berlin, dividing the Soviet-controlled zone of the city from the NATO-controlled ones. Many people died trying to cross the Berlin Wall, to escape from the communist East into Western Europe.

△ *West Berliners wave across the new wall dividing their city. A little later, East German police would throw tear gas grenades over the wall, to prevent even this contact between West and East.*

The Cuban Missile Crisis

Cuba, ruled by Fidel Castro, was a communist outpost just off the coast of the USA. In October 1962, US spy planes discovered that Soviet missiles were being installed in Cuba. The US government of President John F. Kennedy demanded that the Soviet Union withdraw the weapons. The world came close to nuclear war. But, after tense negotiations, the Soviet Union gave way.

◁ *October 1962. During the Cuban Missile Crisis, US President John F. Kennedy makes a TV broadcast from the White House, to announce that US ships would prevent all Soviet military ships from reaching Cuba.*

The USA's war in Vietnam

The 1960s was a troubled decade for the USA. The country was sucked into a major war in Vietnam, which was divided into a communist-ruled state of North Vietnam and a pro-American South Vietnam. Hundreds of thousands of US troops, plus massive air and naval power, were used in an attempt to stop a communist takeover in South Vietnam. By 1970, almost 50,000 young Americans had died in Vietnam, without achieving victory. The war caused bitter controversy in the USA. Many young people joined anti-war demonstrations.

John Levin, a student leader in San Francisco, said:

'We'd been brought up to believe ... that America fought on the side of justice ... So, along with the absolute horror of the war in Vietnam, there was also a feeling of personal betrayal. I remember crying ... late at night in my room, listening to the reports of the war.'

△ *A US soldier in Hue, South Vietnam, comforts a wounded comrade, 1968.*

Assassinations

The most dramatic single event of the decade was the assassination of US President John F. Kennedy in 1963. An official enquiry held that he was killed by a lone sniper, Lee Harvey Oswald – who was shot dead himself, two days after Kennedy's death, while in police custody.

President Kennedy's brother, Robert Kennedy, was also assassinated, in 1968. So was the African American Civil Rights leader, Martin Luther King.

▽ *22 November 1963. The assassination of President Kennedy as he rode through Dallas in an open-topped car was caught on film by an amateur photographer. Kennedy's wife, Jackie (in pink), holds her husband.*

...Newsflash...

Washington DC, 28 August 1963.
Martin Luther King today addressed the largest Civil Rights protest ever, as 200,000 demonstrators responded to his call for a March on Washington. Celebrities including Marlon Brando, Bob Dylan and Judy Garland were there to support the call for equal rights for America's black population. At the Lincoln Memorial, King told the crowd: 'I have a dream that all God's children, black men and white men, Jews and Gentiles, Protestants and Catholics, will be able to join hands ...'

Civil Rights and Black Power

The Civil Rights movement in the USA, led by Martin Luther King, was a campaign for equal rights for African Americans. Many whites in the southern states violently resisted the drive for 'desegregation' – allowing blacks to use the same schools and other public facilities as whites. They also resisted giving blacks the right to vote. By the end of the decade, new laws and direct action by African Americans had largely given blacks the rights they craved. But this did not end racial tension.

At first, most African Americans followed King in his non-violence and his desire for a 'colour-blind' society. Later in the 1960s, the more aggressive Black Power movement emerged. It asserted the distinct qualities of black people. There was a series of large-scale riots in black ghettos in US cities between 1964 and 1968.

▽ *Martin Luther King and his wife lead a Civil Rights march in Alabama, 1965. Inspired by the ideas of Indian campaigner Mahatma Gandhi, King stuck to non-violent methods of protest, even when his enemies resorted to extreme violence.*

South Africa and Rhodesia

At the start of the 1960s, many countries in Africa and the West Indies were still ruled by Europeans as colonies. Most of these colonies became independent in the course of the decade. But in southern Africa white people held out against black rule.

In South Africa, the apartheid system gave whites complete political and economic power over the black majority. Opposition to apartheid was led by the African National Congress (ANC). In 1964 its leader, Nelson Mandela, was sentenced to life imprisonment by a South African court.

In the British colony of Rhodesia (now Zimbabwe), whites declared independence under a white-only government, to prevent Britain holding democratic elections that would have brought in a black government.

Goodbye

De Gaulle, president of France (resigned 1969)

Hello

Mrs Sirimavo Bandaranaike, prime minister of Ceylon, 1960; Jomo Kenyatta, president of Kenya, 1964; Leonid Brezhnev, leader of USSR, 1964

Racism in Europe

Racism was also a problem in Europe. Millions of immigrants from the former colonies started new lives in European countries. They were often not welcomed. In Britain, the government passed laws to limit immigration, but also tried to ban racial prejudice.

▽ *There were separate stairways for whites and non-whites at the railway station in Johannesburg, South Africa.*

...Newsflash...

Pretoria, 14 June 1964. Nelson Mandela, one of the leaders of the struggle against South Africa's racist apartheid regime, was today sentenced to life imprisonment. He has been sent to Robben Island, a prison from which no escape is possible. But Mandela has refused to give up hope. In a powerful speech to the court, he said he still believed in a democratic and free society. 'It is an ideal I hope to live for and achieve,' he said. 'But if needs be, it is an ideal for which I am prepared to die.'

Profile

Indira Gandhi

Indira Gandhi was the daughter of India's first prime minister, Jawaharlal Nehru. She played an important role in the struggle for Indian independence from British rule in the 1940s. By the start of the 1960s, she was president of Congress, India's main political party. In January 1966 she became prime minister.

To have a woman as leader of the government in one of the world's largest countries was a great step forward for women everywhere. Indira Gandhi dominated Indian politics for almost 20 years. She was assassinated in 1984.

Women's rights

Women began to challenge their position in society. In 1963 US feminist Betty Friedan wrote *The Feminine Mystique*, attacking the idea that women should be happy simply being housewives and mothers. She also founded the National Organization for Women (NOW), which campaigned for women's rights in the USA.

A few powerful women leaders emerged, notably Indira Gandhi, prime minister of India from 1966, and Golda Meir, who became Israeli prime minister in 1969.

Liberalization

The 1960s was a decade of liberalization. For example, capital punishment was abolished in Britain in 1967 and put on hold in the USA. Censorship was relaxed. Abortion and homosexuality were legalized. People had different views as to whether these measures were a sign of progress. But certainly times were changing.

▽ *Betty Friedan, a leader of the women's liberation movement in the USA, addresses a meeting in New York.*

A LOOK AT
SCIENCE and TECHNOLOGY
IN THE '60s

Space exploration was the most impressive development in technology in the 1960s. At the start of the decade, no human being had ever left the Earth's atmosphere. By the decade's end, humans had walked on the Moon.

▽ *Soviet leader Nikita Khrushchev (second from right) enjoys the cheers of a crowd for a line of Soviet cosmonauts: (from left) Popovich, Titov, Nikolaev, Gagarin, Tereshkova (the first woman in space, June 1963) and Bykovsky.*

Competition between the USA and the Soviet Union was the driving force behind the Space Race. On 12 April 1961 the Soviet Union put cosmonaut Yuri Gagarin into orbit around the Earth aboard spacecraft Vostok 1. In response, US President John F. Kennedy promised that the USA would land a man on the Moon before the decade was out.

Few people believed it could be done. But the US government invested massive resources in its Apollo space programme. There turned out to be no fundamental obstacles to space travel. On 21 July 1969, US astronaut Neil Armstrong stepped on to the Moon's surface.

Profile

John Glenn

▽ *John Glenn (left) with US Vice-President Lyndon Johnson, 1962.*

US astronaut John Glenn was already 38 years old when he joined the US space programme in 1959. He had fought as a Marine in the Second World War and had flown supersonic aircraft. On 20 February 1962, he became the first American to orbit the Earth. On board the Friendship 7 spacecraft, he completed three orbits before splashing down in the Atlantic. Glenn later entered politics, becoming a senator in 1975. In 1998 he returned to space on board a Shuttle, at the age of 77.

◁ *Crowds watch the Moon landing in 1969, on a large TV screen in Trafalgar Square, London.*

▽ *Apollo 11 astronaut Edwin 'Buzz' Aldrin unpacks equipment on the Moon, 1969.*

Firsts in the Space Race

For a while the Soviet Union stayed ahead in the Space Race. Soviet cosmonaut Alexei Leonov made the first space walk in March 1965, before Edward White became the first American to walk in space in June. The Soviet spacecraft Luna 9 softlanded on the Moon in February 1966, four months ahead of the US Surveyor 1. But the Soviet Union never attempted a programme of manned flights to the Moon. In 1968 three US astronauts made the first manned Moon orbit, and in July 1969, astronauts Aldrin and Armstrong set the US flag on the Moon.

...Newsflash...

20 July 1969. Hundreds of millions of people around the world watched on television tonight as US astronaut Neil Armstrong stepped out of lunar module Eagle and on to the surface of the Moon. Armstrong told the watching millions: 'That's one small step for a man, one giant leap for mankind.' Another member of the Apollo 11 team, Edwin 'Buzz' Aldrin, later joined Armstrong on his historic Moon walk.

◁ *The Early Bird satellite during a test before its launch in 1965.*

Marshall McLuhan, one of the trendiest thinkers of the 1960s, said that television and other electronic communications were recreating the world:

'in the image of a global village'.

Communications

The space programme had a huge impact on communications. But, in the early 1960s, communications were very poor by our standards today. For example, when US President Kennedy was assassinated in 1963, no television pictures from the scene were available in Britain until the following day.

Communications were transformed by satellites. One called Telstar, put into orbit in 1962, allowed the first live TV broadcasts across the Atlantic. But Telstar could only transmit images for a few minutes at a time.

The real turning point was the launch of the Early Bird satellite in 1965. It could be used for communications 24 hours a day. Once a series of similar satellites were in orbit at different locations, instant global communications became a reality.

Computers

Computers were another area that made enormous progress through the space programme, since they were needed to control space vehicles. However, computers were still large and astonishingly expensive machines, only for use by governments and business corporations. Personal computers and computer games did not begin to arrive until the 1970s.

▽ *Loading tapes for storing data on to a one-tonne computer, 1966.*

Technology at home

Technology at home was limited. Most people outside the USA still did not have a telephone at home. In 1964, only about one in 20 US households had colour televisions – which is not surprising since very few television programmes were made in colour. In Britain only the new minority channel, BBC2, broadcast in colour in the 1960s.

Transport

Jet air travel, begun in the 1950s, was developing rapidly. In tune with the space age, Britain and France cooperated to build a supersonic airliner, Concorde. The fastest passenger aircraft ever, it made its first flight in 1969. But in the same year the US Boeing corporation

△ *New models on display at the International Motor Show, 1961.*

Goodbye
Steam trains

Hello
Hovercraft passenger services;
Mont Blanc tunnel;
The QE2 (ship);
Supertankers;
Concorde and jumbo jets

introduced the 'jumbo jet', the Boeing 747. By carrying more passengers in a single aircraft, the jumbo jet helped to make air travel affordable. This turned out to be more important than travelling faster.

The number of cars increased sharply and many new roads were built. Cities were transformed by networks of urban motorways and flyovers. But smaller cars became fashionable and people became more safety-conscious. This was partly due to US campaigner Ralph Nader's book, *Unsafe At Any Speed*, 1965. It attacked the safety record of US motor manufacturers. Car safety belts were invented in the 1960s, but not widely used.

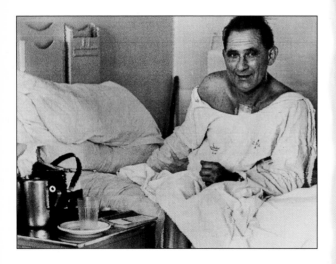

△ *Louis Washkansky survived for 18 days after his heart transplant operation.*

...Newsflash...

Cape Town, 3 December 1967. A South African surgeon, Christiaan Barnard, has carried out the world's first successful heart transplant operation. The patient, a 53-year-old grocer, Louis Washkansky, has been given the heart of a 25-year-old woman who had died in a car accident. It is doubtful that Washkansky will live long, but once this new form of surgery is fully developed, it could save thousands of lives.

Life studies

A revolution in the study of life and the body was beginning with a new understanding of genetics. In 1962, US scientist James Watson and British scientist Francis Crick were awarded the Nobel Prize for their work on DNA, unravelling the genetic code that carries the information to build new organisms, including human beings.

It was a time of major medical progress. In particular, there were advances in dealing with heart disease. Surgeons carried out the first heart bypass operations and inserted the first electronic pacemakers. In 1967, a South African surgeon, Christiaan Barnard, was responsible for the first successful heart transplant operation.

Preventing diseases

There was also progress in the prevention of disease. Campaigns against cigarette smoking got under way, after scientists officially confirmed that there was a link between smoking and cancer.

In many parts of the developing world, vaccination campaigns began to eradicate killer diseases such as smallpox.

▷ *People in the Democratic Republic of the Congo (Zaire) are vaccinated against smallpox.*

Population growth

One result of medical progress was population growth. The steepest rise in world population in human history was taking place, mostly concentrated in the developing countries. Much effort was devoted to ideas for limiting population growth. This was the background to the birth-control pill, developed by American Gregory Pincus in the 1950s and authorized for general use during the 1960s.

The environment

Population growth was one factor behind mounting concern about the human impact on the environment. In her book *Silent Spring*, published in 1963, US naturalist Rachel Carson alerted people to the deadly effect of chemicals such as DDT, sprayed on crops and entering the food chain. The theory of the greenhouse effect, saying that pollution was causing global warming, was first proposed in the 1960s.

There was growing concern about the using up of fossil fuels such as coal and oil. But the 1960s was still a time of technological optimism, when most people believed that science would find a ready answer to such problems. Most advanced countries had large programmes for building nuclear power stations. It was argued that nuclear power would provide a clean, inexhaustible source of energy to replace fossil fuels. This was to prove one of the most over-optimistic of all the 1960s attitudes.

Rachel Carson wrote:

'What we have to face is not an occasional dose of poison which has accidentally got into some article of food, but a persistent and continuous poisoning of the whole human environment.'

▷ *A protective suit for nuclear power station workers, 1964.*

A LOOK AT FASHION

IN THE '60s

The 1960s was the decade when the focus of fashion became what young people were wearing on the street, rather than what was exhibited in haute-couture fashion shows. Also, men became much more style-conscious, where previously fashion had been seen as mostly a woman's concern.

△ Customers at a London café in 1963 listen to and watch a new-style juke box showing moving pictures of the singers.

The early '60s look

Fashions changed a lot in the course of the 1960s. In the early part of the decade, the cool look for men was sharp suits with narrow bottoms to the leg (sometimes called 'drainpipe trousers'). Women tottered along on high 'stiletto' heels, and many wore their hair up in the 'beehive' style. Together the hair and heels made them look taller than they were.

The dresses women wore were designed to emphasize the curves of their hips and bust. Underneath they wore stockings and suspenders, and forcefully uplifting bras. The ideal body shape was thought to be the full figure of the reigning US sex goddess, Marilyn Monroe.

Swinging London

In the mid-'60s, the 'in' look changed radically. There was a fashion revolution that started in London. A group of talented people, including fashion designers Mary Quant and John Stephen,

Mary Quant said:

'I wanted everyone to retain the grace of a child and not to have to become stilted, confined, ugly beings. So I created clothes that worked and moved and allowed people to run, to jump, to leap, to retain their precious freedom.'

◁ Mini-dress and matching-coloured tights designed by Mary Quant.

...Newsflash...

15 April 1966. The USA has discovered the new London of youth and fun. The current edition of the US news magazine *Time* has made 'Swinging London' the subject of its cover story. Most Americans still think of Britain as a conservative place, associated with the Empire and bowler hats. But *Time* reveals that London has become the fashion centre of the world. The magazine writes: 'In this century, every decade has its city ... and for the Sixties that city is London.'

John V. Lindsay, the mayor of New York City, was a typical man of his time in his response to the mini-skirt. He said, jocularly:

'It will enable girls to run faster, and because of it, they may have to!'

▽ *Shoppers in London's Carnaby Street, the centre of 1960s young fashion.*

hairdresser Vidal Sassoon, and photographer David Bailey, made 'Swinging London' the fashion capital of the world. Swinging London generated new fashions that were meant to be fun and were aimed specifically at young people.

The new look

The single most striking feature of the new look was the mini-skirt, and Mary Quant is remembered as the designer most responsible for it. For the first time, women showed their thighs in public. Tights were introduced to replace stockings, as stockings were too revealing under the very short hemlines.

Leading London models such as Jean Shrimpton and Twiggy made fashionable a skinny look with no visible waist or bust. Women wore their hair long and straight with a fringe, or cut short in one of the striking geometrical looks pioneered by Vidal Sassoon.

Designers experimented with fun new materials such as vinyl and PVC, making shiny wet-look raincoats.

As women's skirts got shorter, young men's hair grew longer. Collarless Beatles jackets were the height of fashion. Broad 'kipper' ties came in, and the bottoms of men's trousers began to flare outwards. Black polo-neck sweaters were fashionable, along with hipsters – jeans or trousers with the waistband at hip level.

▽ *Men's hair grew longer and longer through the decade. Here's fashion photographer David Bailey in 1964 ...*

◁ *Jean Shrimpton caused a scandal when she attended a sports event in Australia in 1965, in a mini-dress, and with no hat, gloves or stockings.*

Style wars

Jeans and T-shirts, associated before with manual workers, became the basic clothing of young people across the world. This was part of a general revolt against formality. Many young men rejected suits and ties as too stuffy and conventional. David Bailey wore jeans at his wedding to the French film star Catherine Deneuve. Rolling Stones singer Mick Jagger got married in corduroy trousers and a sweater.

Earlier fashions had been designed to make men and women look different. But from the mid-1960s, many fashions were 'uni-sex'. With some women having short hair, and some men long hair, and both sexes wearing hipster jeans and T-shirts, it was often quite difficult to tell the sexes apart. Many older people found this very disturbing.

Fashion became a battleground between young and old. Long hair for boys shocked traditionalists as much as the mini-skirt.

Profile

Twiggy

Sixties model Twiggy (real name Lesley Hornby) was born in the London suburb of Neasden in 1949. She was rejected by modelling schools because she was too short and had too narrow hips. But this setback was shortlived, for she was still only 16 when the London press discovered her as 'the face of 1966'. She soon made a triumphant visit to the USA where her youthful charm, startling figure and ultra-modish short haircut caused a sensation. Twiggy remained a fashionable figure into the 1970s.

Some schools tried to force pupils to abandon the fashions with rules that a girl's skirt hem must touch the ground when she knelt, or that a boy's hair must not reach further than the top back of his collar. There was opposition to the new styles in the adult world too. For example, women in fashionable trouser suits were refused entry to some restaurants and clubs.

▷ *Trouser suits modelled in London, 1967.*

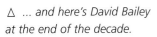

△ *... and here's David Bailey at the end of the decade.*

Afghans and Afros

Towards the end of the 1960s, more shifts in style took place. The spreading influence of the Hippie movement led to the wearing of embroidered blouses, Afghan coats and ethnic skirts, beads and even cow bells. Young men's hair became even longer, and beards and moustaches grew in popularity. But the decade-long trend towards shorter hemlines stopped. Medium-length 'midi-skirts' and ankle-length 'maxi-skirts' came in alongside the mini. Some women wore a long maxi-coat over a mini-skirt.

◁ Tie-dyed trousers and an Afghan waistcoat for an open-air festival, 1967.

▷ Dancing at a Los Angeles club, body painted with psychedelic designs under a plastic dress.

For African Americans, the 1960s also marked a style revolution, though of a different kind. At the start of the decade, most African Americans liked to be as 'yellow' as possible – that is, pale rather than dark-skinned. They also used to straighten their hair, taking out the crimp natural to African hair. But the 'black is beautiful' slogan of the second half of the 1960s led many African Americans to change their attitude to their looks. The more radical adopted Afro hairstyles designed to emphasize their ethnic origins. Some also wore African-style brightly-patterned fabrics. Without going that far, most African Americans were influenced by the trend to take pride in their ethnic identity.

◁ An Afro hairstyle worn by Marsha Hunt.

A LOOK AT
MUSIC
IN THE '60s

Most music fans look back on the 1960s as a golden age of pop. Heroes of the decade, such as the Beatles, Bob Dylan, Jimi Hendrix and Jim Morrison, are still revered by many today. Such gifted individuals gave pop music a new status as a key element in modern cultural life.

▽ *Young people study album covers in a record shop in 1965.*

A large youth market for records had developed for the first time in the 1950s, as young people came to have more spending money. The new recording business grew phenomenally in the 1960s. By 1967, record sales in the USA were worth more than $1 billion a year. This was more than double the value of record sales ten years earlier.

The records were all shiny vinyl discs. (Cassettes only began to come in at the very end of the decade.) Records were often released in two versions, mono and stereo. Early in the decade, only a minority of people had stereo equipment. The sound quality available to most listeners was quite poor.

Goodbye
Rock'n'roll;
Elvis Presley

Hello
Pop festivals;
light shows;
Beatlemania;
Motown

Their record players had small built-in speakers, and the records gathered dust and got scratched. Yet listening through the crackle and hiss of the needle finding its way along the grooves of the record, young people found amazing excitement in the fresh new music that was being made.

Profile

Joan Baez

Joan Baez, seen here with Bob Dylan with whom she was closely associated, was a leading figure on the folk protest scene in the 1960s. Her beautiful voice won her a huge following, with songs such as 'What have they done to the rain?' The daughter of a Mexican American scientist, she was a dedicated campaigner against racism and the USA's war in Vietnam. She was twice jailed for her anti-war protests, when she joined demonstrators blocking the way into induction centres, where young Americans were sent to join the army.

Motown and folk protest

At the start of the 1960s, pop was at a low point. The rock'n'roll boom of the 1950s, led by the likes of Elvis Presley and Bill Haley, had run out of steam. But in Detroit, a former car worker, Berry Gordy Jr, launched the Motown label in 1960. With performers such as Diana Ross (in the Supremes), Stevie Wonder and Marvin Gaye, Motown was soon turning out a string of hits that were to be the top dance music of the decade.

Another strand in the creation of the 1960s music scene was the folk protest music of singer-songwriters such as Bob Dylan and Joan Baez. In the early 1960s, they performed songs you couldn't dance to – accompanied by acoustic guitar – to quiet, respectful white audiences in New York or at the annual Newport Folk festival. But by 1965 folk had gone hip. Braving the hostility of his dedicated folk fans, Dylan got an electric backing band and produced songs that were close to being the first rap.

▽ *The Supremes. Diana Ross is on the left.*

Rule Britannia

The main influence that turned Bob Dylan electric was the British bands which burst onto the scene from 1963. Until this time, most British pop had been a weak imitation of American music. But British youth culture was beginning to bubble with fresh ideas in music and fashion. In 1962, a well-established Liverpool band, the Beatles, recorded their first national hit single, 'Love Me Do'. Within a year, 'Beatlemania' had swept Britain. In scenes of mass hysteria, crowds of screaming teenagers mobbed the 'Moptops' wherever they went. In 1964, the Beatles went on a tour of the USA, and received a similar welcome there.

▷ *The Beatles arrive in the USA, 1964.*

...Newsflash...

9 February 1964. Britain's top pop group, the Beatles, have arrived in the USA and are taking the country by storm. When the Fab Four touched down at New York's Kennedy Airport two days ago, thousands of screaming fans had turned up to give them a big welcome. Their song 'I want to hold your hand' is already top of the Hot 100 singles chart, and their appearance on *The Ed Sullivan Show* tonight has drawn a record TV audience of 73 million. For the first time, Americans are rocking to a British beat.

" "

According to Beatle Paul McCartney, the Beatles themselves were often shocked at how seriously people took them. Of fans who blamed the Beatles for failing to change the world, he said:

'I don't really think that we thought that we were going to change the world as much as you thought we were going to change the world.'

In the wake of the Beatles, a series of British bands stormed the pop charts on both sides of the Atlantic: the Rolling Stones, Gerry and the Pacemakers, the Kinks, the Animals and the Who. The Beatles themselves split up in 1970, to pursue solo careers. The US entertainment industry paid them the compliment of imitation, manufacturing a band, the Monkees, modelled on the Beatles, for a TV series.

△ *The Kinks, 1968.*

Profile

Jimi Hendrix

Born in Seattle, Washington, Jimi Hendrix was a paratrooper in the US army before making his living as a musician. In 1967 he shot to fame after appearing at the Monterey Pop Festival with his band, the Jimi Hendrix Experience. He was a guitar player of genius, who constantly experimented with imaginative new sounds. He also developed a wild stage act that sometimes ended with him setting his guitar on fire. He died in London in September 1970, two months before his 28th birthday.

Voices of a generation

The new British sound was fresh, irreverent and fun. But 1960s pop music soon began to get heavier. The influences of the Hippie drug culture and of youth protest began to be felt. Pop stars became conscious of being the 'voice of a generation', often at odds with the authorities. They wrote their own material, creating lyrics that were far removed from the simple 'luv' songs of most previous pop.

Unusual instruments such as the sitar appeared on pop records, as did strange electronic effects. Bands such as Cream and the Jimi Hendrix Experience explored the potential of the electric guitar to the limits in often rambling solos. The Beatles' 1967 album 'Sergeant Pepper's Lonely Hearts Club Band' started a new tradition of 'theme' albums – linked tracks instead of a collection of singles.

△ *Listening to one of the bands at Woodstock, 1969.*

Festival time

In 1967 the era of open-air pop festivals began. It reached its peak in the Woodstock festival in the USA in 1969 and the Isle of Wight festival in England in 1970. These events were much hyped.

...Newsflash...

Bethel, 17 August 1969. Some 400,000 young people have swarmed to the small town of Bethel in New York State for the Woodstock Music and Arts Fair. They have been drawn by a list of performers that includes Jefferson Airplane, the Who, Janis Joplin, and Crosby, Stills, Nash and Young. The weekend is being hailed as a triumphant celebration of youth culture. Despite traffic jams, shortages of food and water, and torrential rain, everyone seems to be having a good time.

1960s pop festivals were almost all badly organized, with poor facilities and inadequate sound systems. John Leaver, who worked on an 'underground' magazine, remembers:

'I'm sitting in the middle of a field with 50,000 other people and the Grateful Dead are half a mile away, and I'm thinking, "I must be having fun".'

Listening to bands such as Jefferson Airplane, the Grateful Dead and the Doors, the young generation was supposed to experience itself as a 'counter-culture' of peace and love, opposed to the money-obsessed, war-making culture of its parents. But for most who went, it was more a fun way of passing a weekend.

▽ *The Grateful Dead, Woodstock, 1969.*

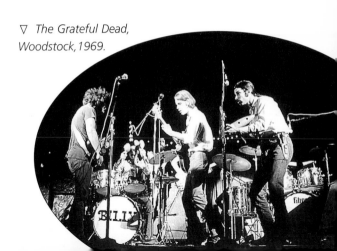

A LOOK AT
ART and ARCHITECTURE
IN THE '60s

In the 1960s many painters and sculptors wanted to take part in the fun and glamour of popular culture. They created a new movement called Pop art, which was up-to-date, witty and accessible.

Pop art

Pop art drew much of its inspiration from advertizing, supermarket goods, movies and comic books. It first hit the headlines in 1962, when American artist Andy Warhol exhibited reproductions of Campbell's soup cans. Warhol's other works included repeated images of pop idols such as Elvis Presley and Marilyn Monroe. Other American Pop artists included Roy Lichtenstein and Claes Oldenburg.

Pop art also flourished in Britain, with artists such as David Hockney, Richard Hamilton and Peter Blake. In the second half of the 1960s, Hockney moved to California, where he made a famous series of paintings of swimming pools.

❝ ❞

Pop art marked a real change in attitude by the art world. Artists began to take popular culture seriously, but to take themselves less seriously. British Pop artist Richard Hamilton said his art was:

'popular, transient, expendable, low-cost, mass-produced, young, witty, sexy, gimmicky, glamorous and Big Business.'

▽ Roy Lichtenstein made art, such as 'Whaam!' (1963), out of blown-up images from comic strips. It is said that he was first inspired by one of his children who pointed to a comic book and said, 'I bet you can't paint as good as that!'

Profile

Andy Warhol

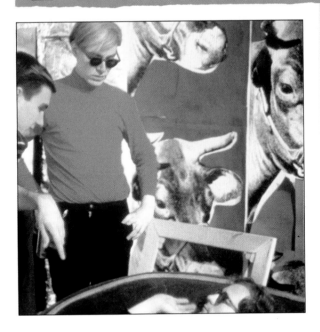

US Pop artist Andy Warhol caused a sensation in 1962 when he exhibited pictures of Campbell's soup cans in an art gallery. He called his New York studio 'The Factory' and set out to mass-produce art, as factories mass-produced identical consumer goods.

Warhol also made strange movies – one of them, called *Sleep*, showed a man sleeping for six hours – and promoted a rock group, Velvet Underground. In 1968 he was shot and seriously wounded by Valerie Solanas, founder of the Society for Cutting Up Men (SCUM). Warhol died in 1987.

△ *Andy Warhol, in red, and friends in his studio.*

▽ *Swedish-born American artist Claes Oldenburg produced giant sculptures of food, such as ice-cream cones and hamburgers, and 'soft sculptures' of normally hard objects, like this Soft Drum Kit of 1967. It is made of vinyl and canvas, filled with expanded polystyrene chips.*

Even artists who were not part of the Pop art movement often reacted to the sense of colour and modernity bursting into 1960s life. In Britain, for example, sculpture was dominated at first by the sombre bronze sculptures of Henry Moore, based on natural forms. But Moore's influence waned in the 1960s and the rising star was Anthony Caro, who produced sculptures in bright colours, using manufactured materials such as aluminium tubes and steel plates. Caro said he wanted to produce sculptures that had absolutely nothing to do with the art of the past.

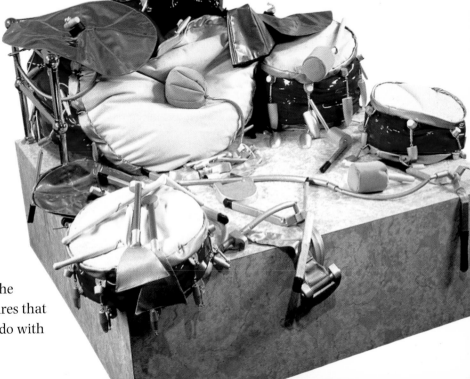

Making it happen

Another feature of 1960s art was the 'happening'. This was a bizarre or provocative event presented as a work of art. French artist Yves Klein, for example, smeared naked women with paint and dragged them over a canvas, while refined music was played and a formally dressed audience looked on. Another artist who created happenings was Yoko Ono, who later married Beatle John Lennon. On one occasion she sat on stage and members of the audience were invited to come up to cut off pieces of her dress with scissors.

Yoko Ono's involvement with the Beatles was one example of how the world of art crossed over with pop music and fashion in the 1960s. Andy Warhol promoted his own rock band, Velvet Underground, featuring singer Lou Reed. By 1965 the Beatles were mixing in the arty world of Swinging London, a setting far removed from their Liverpool working-class roots. The cover for the Beatles' 'Sergeant Pepper's Lonely Hearts Club Band' album was designed by Pop artist Peter Blake.

△ An Op art dress by an Italian designer is modelled in Milan in 1966.

Mary Quant and other fashion designers produced a range of black-and-white clothes based on Op art. This was an art movement exploiting visual illusions created by strange abstract patterns.

◁ The Beatles' Bentley was painted with psychedelic designs.

Building styles

Most 1960s architecture was in the 'modernist' style that had triumphed across the globe since the Second World War. In almost every city and every country, high-rise concrete and glass buildings were going up, designed in a functional style that avoided fussy details or anything that might make a link to the architecture of the past. Tall buildings such as London's Centre Point and Post Office Tower transformed skylines in previously low-rise cities.

Ordinary people always had problems with this style of architecture, especially when they were asked to live in high-rise buildings on council estates or housing projects. The era of this international style was coming to an end. It would not be long before the authorities started knocking down high-rise blocks, and architects began designing wacky buildings that were fun again.

▽ *High-rise flats in London.*

" "

Nigel Waymouth designed psychedelic posters in the 1960s. He later explained:

'Before that fly-posters were very dull ... We decided to paint pictures and use the gaudiest and the brightest colours, rainbow colours, silver, gold ... It was great fun and it brightened up all those tatty corrugated iron fences.'

Psychedelia

In the second half of the 1960s, youth culture produced its own art style, known as psychedelia. American artist Milton Glaser was the finest exponent of psychedelic posters and album covers in the later 1960s. With its bright colours and swirly patterns, psychedelia was supposed to represent mind-altering drug experiences.

A LOOK AT
SPORT
IN THE '60s

In the 1960s, sport became more commercial. It also became more involved with political issues, especially the question of equal rights for black people. But what really mattered for sports fans, as usual, were the outstanding performances of supremely talented individuals.

When the 1960s began, there were still sports where the ideal of amateurism was upheld – the principle that people should not earn money from their sport. The Wimbledon tennis tournament, for example, was only open to amateur players. But more and more of the

▽ Abebe Bikila, from Ethiopia, won the marathon at the Olympic Games in Rome, 1960. He ran the race barefoot.

Profile

Muhammad Ali

Possibly the greatest boxer of all time, Muhammad Ali first made his mark as an amateur, winning a gold medal at the 1960 Rome Olympics. At that time he was known as Cassius Clay. He changed his name to Muhammad Ali after joining the black Muslim movement, the 'Nation of Islam', in 1964. In the same year he became world heavyweight champion. Ali had his title taken away in 1967 after he refused to serve in the US army in protest at the Vietnam war. He won the title back twice in the 1970s.

◁ November 1965: Muhammad Ali (left) in a match with Floyd Patterson.

...Newsflash...

Mexico City, October 1968.
American 200-metre gold medallist Tommie Smith and bronze winner John Carlos have been suspended from the Olympics and thrown out of the Olympic village after a sensational demonstration in favour of black rights in the USA. US athletics officials were stunned as the pair bowed their heads and raised black-gloved fists in the Black Power salute after receiving their medals. It was a deliberate gesture of solidarity with African Americans fighting against what they see as oppression and racism in the USA. The authorities have made it clear that the two athletes will be made to pay dearly for their political gesture.

△ *Having received their medals at the Mexico Olympics. African American athletes Tommie Smith and John Carlos gave Black Power salutes while the US national anthem was played. For doing so they were banned from the USA's team.*

top tennis stars became professionals, and consequently could not play at Wimbledon. In 1968, the International Lawn Tennis Association was forced to abolish the distinction between amateurs and professionals, opening Wimbledon to all.

In sports that had long been big business, such as major league baseball and soccer, the star players began to take a larger cut of the profits. In 1960, top British soccer players earned little more than an average working man. By the end of the decade stars such as Manchester United's George Best had become wealthy high earners. American football set out to increase its profits by starting the Super Bowl in 1967.

Race and sport

The question of black rights was bound to have an impact on sport because so many top performers were black. South Africa's racist policies led to a movement for the country to be banned from world sport. The climax came when the South Africans themselves refused to compete against non-whites.

In the USA, sports personalities such as boxer Cassius Clay (Muhammad Ali) and athletes Tommie Smith and John Carlos became involved in the struggle for black rights.

ENGLAND 3 GERMANY W. 2

◁ In the 1966 World Cup final between England and Germany, Geoff Hurst (right) shoots to score the fourth goal for England.

For the English, the greatest sports event of the decade was the England football team winning the World Cup at Wembley in 1966.

Americans dominated golf. Arnold Palmer was the leading golfer at the start of the decade, but in 1962 a young fellow-American, Jack Nicklaus, won his first major tournament. By the end of the decade Nicklaus was well on his way to becoming the most successful golfer of all time.

At the Rome Olympics in 1960, Ethiopian Abebe Bikila astonished the crowds by winning the marathon barefoot. He won again at the Tokyo Olympics in 1964 – the first person to gain two consecutive marathon golds.

Known as the 'Golden Bear' because he was 'large, strong, blond, and maybe a little growly', Jack Nicklaus wrote that:

'In golf, almost everyone loses a whole lot more than he wins ... The most obvious reason is surely the huge role luck plays in golf.'

▷ Carrying the Olympic flame at the Tokyo Olympics in 1964 was student Yoshinori Sakai. He was born on 6 August 1945, the day that the atomic bomb was dropped on the Japanese city of Hiroshima.

Profile

Billie Jean King

Born in California in 1943, Billie Jean King (born Billie Jean Moffitt) shone through in the 1960s as the top woman tennis star of her generation. She won her first Wimbledon women's singles title in 1966, beating Maria Bueno in the final, and retained the title for the next two years.

King's powerful, aggressive style of play challenged the assumption that men's tennis was better than women's. She remained a leading player throughout the 1970s, winning the Wimbledon singles title three more times.

△ Billie Jean King (then Billie Jean Moffitt), June 1962.

The Mexico Olympics in 1968 produced some outstanding records, partly because the games were held at high altitude, aiding performances. US athlete Bob Beamon broke the world long jump record by 55 centimetres, setting a record that lasted until 1991. Another US athlete, Dick Fosbury, won the high jump gold with a revolutionary style of jump, known as the Fosbury Flop.

Australians ruled in tennis, with Rod Laver the leading male player and Margaret Court the leading female star. However, Court's dominance was challenged in the later 1960s by the young American Billie Jean King.

A LOOK AT
LEISURE and ENTERTAINMENT
IN THE '60s

In the 1960s, watching television was by far the most popular leisure activity. It was still a relatively novel experience, as television broadcasting had not really got going until the 1950s. There were fewer TV channels than there are today and most people had only small black-and-white TV sets. But the poor picture quality and limited choice of programmes did not lessen viewers' fascination.

Families gathered around their TVs to watch Westerns such as *Rawhide* and *Bonanza*, thriller series such as *The Man From UNCLE*, *The Avengers* and *The Fugitive*, and the science fiction series *Star Trek* and, in Britain, *Dr Who*. Classic comedies included *The Addams Family*, *The Munsters*, *The Beverly Hillbillies* and *Bewitched*.

▽ In 'The Fugitive', a character called Dr Richard Kimble was on the run from a policeman, after the murder of his wife, and always chasing the real murderer – the one-armed man shown here.

Hello Z Cars, The Avengers, Coronation Street, 1960; The Flintstones, 1961; Steptoe and Son, 1962; Dr Who, 1963; Thunderbirds, The Magic Roundabout, 1965; Star Trek, Till Death Us Do Part, 1966; Monty Python's Flying Circus, 1969

The steamy soap *Peyton Place* starred future film stars Mia Farrow and Ryan O'Neal. British TV hits ranged from the start of *Coronation Street*, still on screen today, to nostalgia series such as *The Forsyte Saga*.

The irreverent side of the 1960s was represented by programmes such as the British satire show *That Was The Week That Was* and the zany US comedy review *The Rowan and Martin Laugh-In*, which made Goldie Hawn a star. One of its catchphrases was 'Sock it to me!'

The poet and critic T.S. Eliot wrote in the 'New York Post' in September 1963 that television:

'permits millions of people to listen to the same joke at the same time, and yet remain lonesome.'

▷ *Goldie Hawn and Sammy Davis on the set of the US comedy show, 'The Rowan and Martin Laugh-In', October 1968.*

Television also brought events of the day into people's homes with a new vividness. During the Vietnam war, people saw images of the death and destruction on their TV sets every evening. Only 20 years earlier, during the Second World War, people had had to rely on newspaper reports and photos and newsreels at the cinema.

▽ *The Monkees pop group (left to right: Davy Jones, Micky Dolenz, Peter Tork and Mike Nesmith) was formed especially for a TV series, full of zany action.*

From its start in 1966, each episode of 'Star Trek' began with the words:

'Space – the final frontier. These are the voyages of the starship Enterprise. Its five-year mission: to explore strange new worlds, to seek out new life and new civilizations, to boldly go where no man has gone before.'

At the movies

At the start of the 1960s, the cinema was in crisis through losing customers to television. The movie companies tried to attract people away from their black-and-white TV sets by presenting a lavish visual spectacle, making wide-screen epics such as *Cleopatra*, *Lawrence of Arabia* and *Dr Zhivago*. Later in the decade, Hollywood began to lure audiences with movies that had a degree of explicit sex and violence in them that was beyond anything allowed on television.

Westerns were big in the 1960s, from *The Magnificent Seven* in 1960 to the violent Italian-made 'spaghetti Westerns' such as *A Fistful of Dollars*, starring Clint Eastwood, and the comedy Western *Butch Cassidy and*

the Sundance Kid, starring Paul Newman and Robert Redford, in 1969.

▽ *In 'Butch Cassidy and the Sundance Kid', American society is seen through the outlaw's point of view.*

Profile

Sidney Poitier

Sometimes described as the first black superstar, Sidney Poitier was called upon whenever the movies needed a worthy, charming, courageous African American 'Mr Clean'. In 1964 he became the first black performer to win an Academy Award for best actor, for his role in *Lilies of the Field*. His most memorable film role was as a sophisticated black detective, Virgil Tibbs, in the 1967 thriller *In the Heat of the Night*. Set in a small town in Mississippi, the film is a powerful study of racial prejudice.

Profile

Julie Christie

Born in 1940, British actress Julie Christie had her first starring role in the film *Billy Liar* in 1963. She was soon seen as someone who typically represented the spirit of Swinging London, with its mini-skirts and liberated young women. In 1965 she won an Academy Award for her part as a spoilt trendy model in *Darling*. Christie went on to star in other successful movies including *Dr Zhivago*, where she played opposite a heart-throb of the period, Omar Sharif, and *Far from the Madding Crowd*.

◁ *Christie in the 1966 film 'Fahrenheit 451'.*

Special effects made great strides in Stanley Kubrick's science fiction movie *2001: A Space Odyssey*. Disney feature-length cartoons included *The Jungle Book*, the first Disney cartoon to have a pop-music soundtrack.

▽ *Julie Andrews sings 'My Favourite Things' in the 1965 musical 'The Sound of Music'.*

British films and stars were in vogue. James Bond movies, starring Sean Connery, were immensely successful. The first was *Dr No* in 1962. Other spy movies included *The Ipcress File*, starring Michael Caine. Julie Andrews was a hit in the musicals *The Sound of Music* and *Mary Poppins*. Comedian Peter Sellars starred in *Dr Strangelove* and the Pink Panther movies. The Beatles made their own cartoon feature film, *Yellow Submarine*, as well as starring in *A Hard Day's Night* and *Help!*

Throughout the 1960s, censorship became steadily less heavy-handed. Many older people complained about the increasing amount of explicit sex and foul language found both on television and in the cinema. Yet even by the end of the decade, there was nothing like as much nudity or obscenity allowed on screens as we are used to today.

Dance

Dance crazes came and went through the decade. The most famous of them was the Twist, introduced by singer Chubby Checker in 1961. As the decade progressed, dancing became less structured, with more free self-expression. Discos were livened up with rather primitive 'psychedelic' light shows and strobes.

▷ *Americans dance the Twist for a crowd of onlookers.*

Other youth activities

In the early 1960s, the coolest youth activities in the USA were driving hot rods – souped-up second-hand cars – and surfing. But the influence of the Hippie revolution made young people more laid back. Throwing a frisbee was the coolest late-1960s cult, because it was seen as non-competitive and peaceful, ideal for spaced-out afternoons in the park.

Open-air music festivals became larger and more frequent as the decade went on, culminating in the famous Woodstock festival in 1969. They were a prime opportunity for young people to explore sexual experiences and experiment with 'consciousness-expanding' drugs such as cannabis and LSD (or 'Acid').

Amsterdam and Copenhagen became popular holiday destinations for the young, because of their tolerant attitude towards drugs. Thousands of young people also at least once followed the 'Hippie trail' – the long overland route from Europe to Afghanistan and India.

Travel

Most young people either hitch-hiked or travelled by bus or train. Although young Americans could afford a one-off transatlantic flight to 'do' Europe, travelling by air was simply too expensive for most students most of the time. Yet air travel was becoming increasingly available to ordinary people. For example, the British working class began to take cheap package holidays on the Costa

Brava or in Majorca, whereas before only the well-off middle classes had holidayed abroad.

Childhood in the 1960s

For children there were, relative to today, few interesting things to do in the 1960s. Go-karting was a craze of the time. Scalextric, with electric racing cars guided round a track by hand-held controls, was the most hi-tech toy available.

Lego, invented in the 1950s, was becoming popular, although in a primitive form with little more than rectangular blocks in different colours. Barbie dolls and Action Man toys both became popular for the first time in the 1960s. Primitive skateboards – flat wooden boards pedalled along with the free foot like a scooter – had existed for a decade in the USA, but were little used. For many

▽ *The start of a 20-lap go-kart race.*

children their most prized possession was a bicycle – ridden without a crash helmet. In the absence of videos, video games, home computers and leisure parks, the revolution in childhood was still to happen.

▽ *On the 'Hippie trail' in Kathmandu, Nepal.*

A British student describes a holiday in 1968:

'I set off to hitch-hike around Europe with a small rucksack, a sleeping bag, and £50 for six weeks' holiday. Hitch-hiking could be tough. Because of my long hair, lots of drivers were aggressive, shouted things or made signs. But I met other young people like myself, slept on beaches and in parks, had adventures. And I arrived back home with 1s 6d in my pocket.'

Date List

1960

3 February ▷ British Prime Minister Harold Macmillan makes a speech declaring that 'the wind of change is blowing through Africa'. Britain, France and Belgium all begin a rapid withdrawal from their African colonies.

1 May ▷ An American U2 spy plane piloted by Gary Powers is shot down over the Soviet Union.

June ▷ The Motown record label is launched in Detroit.

1 October ▷ Britain grants independence to Nigeria. Britain's other African colonies become independent over the following five years.

8 November ▷ John F. Kennedy wins the US presidential election. Aged 43, he is the youngest ever US president.

Also in 1960 ... ▷ The US Food and Drug Administration approves the birth-control pill for sale in the USA.

1961

12 April ▷ Soviet cosmonaut Yuri Gagarin becomes the first man in space, orbiting the Earth on a 108-minute flight.

13 August ▷ Berlin is divided in two as the building of a wall begins, separating the communist East from West Berlin.

1962

January ▷ The Twist emerges as the biggest dance craze for many years.

20 February ▷ John Glenn becomes the first American to orbit the Earth.

22 October ▷ The Cuban missile crisis begins when President Kennedy announces that the Soviet Union is stationing nuclear missiles in Cuba. The crisis eventually ends with the dismantling of the Soviet missile sites.

10 July ▷ The communications satellite Telstar is launched. It allows the first broadcast of television pictures across the Atlantic.

31 October ▷ Pop art hits the headlines as a major exhibition opens in New York, including Andy Warhol's pictures of Campbell's soup cans.

1963

May ▷ The Beatles release their first album, *Please Please Me*.

5 June ▷ The British Defence Minister John Profumo is forced to resign after a scandal involving callgirl Christine Keeler.

28 August ▷ More than 200,000 people, led by Martin Luther King, demonstrate for Civil Rights in the March on Washington.

22 November ▷ President Kennedy is assassinated in Dallas, Texas.

Also in 1963 ... ▷ Betty Friedan publishes *The Feminine Mystique*, seen as the starting point of the Women's Movement.

and ... ▷ Rachel Carson publishes *The Silent Spring*, pointing out the dangers of the use of pesticides in farming.

1964

7 February ▷ The Beatles begin their triumphant first visit to the USA.

25 February ▷ Cassius Clay (Muhammad Ali) defeats Sonny Liston to become world heavyweight boxing champion.

14 June ▷ South African anti-apartheid leader Nelson Mandela is sentenced to life imprisonment for treason.

1965

8 March ▷ US combat troops are sent into South Vietnam to fight communist guerrillas.

18 March ▷ Soviet cosmonaut Alexei Leonov makes the first spacewalk.

Also in 1965 ... ▷ The mini-skirt, first sold in Mary Quant's Chelsea boutique, takes the fashion world by storm.

1966

April ▷ *Time* magazine declares that the grooviest city in the world is 'Swinging London'.

May ▷ Mass parades of young Red Guards march through Peking as China's Cultural Revolution gets under way.

2 July ▷ Billie Jean King wins her first Wimbledon singles title.

30 July ▷ England's footballers win the World Cup at Wembley, beating West Germany 4-2 after extra time.

Also in 1966 ... ▷ The sci-fi series *Star Trek* appears for the first time on US television.

1967

15 January ▷ American football's first Superbowl is won by the Green Bay Packers.

19 March ▷ An oil tanker, the *Torrey Canyon*, runs on to rocks off Cornwall, spilling vast quantities of crude oil into the sea.

1 June ▷ The Beatles' concept album *Sergeant Pepper's Lonely Hearts Club Band* is released.

5-10 June ▷ Israel defeats its Arab neighbours in the Six-Day War.

18 June ▷ Jimi Hendrix achieves stardom at the Monterey open-air pop festival.

10 October ▷ The body of Latin American revolutionary leader Che Guevara is displayed to the world's press. He was killed trying to start an uprising in Bolivia.

3 December ▷ The world's first successful heart transplant operation is carried out by Dr Christiaan Barnard in Cape Town.

1968

4 April ▷ Civil Rights leader Martin Luther King is assassinated at a motel in Memphis, Tennessee.

10 May ▷ Students battle with police in Paris on the 'Night of the Barricades'. The riots spark a student revolt and general strike that bring France to a halt for a month.

5 June ▷ Robert Kennedy, younger brother of President John F. Kennedy, is shot dead by a Palestinian, Sirhan Sirhan.

21 August ▷ The Soviet Union and some of its allies invade Czechoslovakia to end the experiment with liberal communism known as the 'Prague Spring'.

October ▷ The Olympic Games are held in Mexico. American sprinters Tommie Smith and John Carlos are expelled for giving the Black Power salute.

1969

2 March ▷ The supersonic airliner Concorde makes its maiden flight.

20 July ▷ Neil Armstrong is the first man to set foot on the Moon in the successful Apollo 11 mission.

14 August ▷ British troops are sent on to the streets of Northern Ireland to restore order after violence flares up between Protestants and Catholics.

17 August ▷ The Woodstock festival ends after three days of music by Jefferson Airplane, Janis Joplin, the Who, Jimi Hendrix, and many others.

Glossary

ANC

ANC stands for African National Congress, the organization that led the resistance to apartheid in South Africa. After 1994, the ANC became the leading party in the post-apartheid South African government.

apartheid

Apartheid was the system of racial segregation operated by the white rulers of South Africa between 1949 and 1992.

Black Power

Black Power was a loosely structured movement that developed among African Americans in the second half of the 1960s. It suggested that black people should assert their own values rather than seeking integration in white society. Black Power radicals also believed that the use of force was often justified, especially in self-defence.

boutique

A small shop selling fashionable clothes.

capital punishment

The punishment of a crime by death.

Carnaby Street

A street in London's West End where many trendy clothes shops for young people were set up in the 1960s.

CIA

CIA stands for the Central Intelligence Agency, the US organization responsible for spying and other secret activities against the USA's enemies.

Cold War

The Cold War was the armed confrontation between the USA and its allies on one side, and the Soviet Union and its allies on the other, which lasted from the late 1940s to the late 1980s.

communism

Communism is a political and economic system which was first established in the Soviet Union and spread from there to many other countries. Under this system, a single party ruled without tolerating any opposition, and industry and agriculture were controlled by the state.

DDT

An insecticide known to cause long-term damage to animals and humans when used in farming.

flower power

The Hippie belief in changing the world through peace and love.

folk protest

A type of music popular in the early 1960s, using an American folk song style to present lyrics protesting against war, nuclear weapons and racial prejudice.

generation gap

The difference in attitudes, values and behaviour between adults and young people. The generation gap existed in acute form in the 1960s.

Hippie

Hippie is a term used for people in the 1960s who rejected conventional society because of its obsession with work and money. Hippies advocated 'peace and love' and experimented with mind-altering drugs.

Iron Curtain

The Iron Curtain was a term used for the fortified line that divided Western Europe from communist-controlled Eastern Europe from the late 1940s to the late 1980s.

KGB

Soviet secret police and spying organization.

Motown

African American record label based in the car-making city of Detroit. The name was derived from Detroit's nickname, 'Motor Town'.

Nation of Islam

African American movement preaching the Islamic religion and promoting specifically black values against white society.

NATO

NATO stands for the North Atlantic Treaty Organization, an alliance set up in 1949 by the USA and its West European allies to oppose the power of the Soviet Union.

Prague Spring

An attempt in early 1968 to create a liberal form of communism in Czechoslovakia.

psychedelic

A term used for drugs such as LSD that produce hallucinations or altered visual perceptions. The use of the word was extended to refer to kinds of painting and clothes design using swirly, brightly-coloured patterns.

PVC

PVC stands for polyvinyl chloride, a kind of plastic.

satire

The use of humour to ridicule politicians and criticize social customs or attitudes.

spaghetti Western

A term used for movies about American cowboys that were made in Europe by Italian filmmakers. Spaghetti Westerns were hugely popular in the 1960s, beginning with Sergio Leone's *A Fistful of Dollars* (1964), which starred Clint Eastwood.

Summer of Love

A name given to the summer of 1967, because of the huge number of Hippie-influenced open-air festivals, Be-Ins and Love-Ins that were held then.

Resources

Books

One good start to reading on the 1960s could be dipping into Jonathon Green's *Days in the Life* (Heinemann-Mandarin, 1988), a series of fascinating snippets from interviews with hundreds of people, both famous and unknown, who were part of the London scene.

Or try Ian MacDonald's *Revolution in the Head* (London, Fourth Estate, 1994), an attempt to understand the new thinking of youth in the 1960s through Beatles' lyrics.

Among novels that help grasp what the 1960s were about, *One Flew Over the Cuckoo's Nest* by Ken Kesey stands out, with its vision of society as a madhouse we need to escape from.

James Baldwin's *Another Country*, first published in 1963, gives one black take on the 1960s.

In a lighter vein, 1960s spy stories such as John Le Carré's *The Spy Who Came in from the Cold* and Len Deighton's *Funeral in Berlin* give a good feel of the Cold War side of the decade.

Thomas Pynchon's *Vineland* is a recent attempt to describe being young and radical in the decade of protest.

Tom Wolfe's *The Electric Kool-Aid Acid Test* is a classic book about the '60s written in the '60s – it looks at the wildest side of the drug-taking West Coast scene.

An even more extreme, hyped-up view of the drug scene is provided by Hunter S. Thompson's *Fear and Loathing in Las Vegas* (1972), in which two deranged Hippies go on an outing.

Australian journalist Richard Neville has written an enjoyable retrospective view of London in the late 1960s, *Hippie Hippie Shake* (London, Bloomsbury, 1995).

The radical political scene of anti-war protest is brilliantly captured in Norman Mailer's two 1960s classics *The Armies of the Night* and *Miami Beach and the Siege of Chicago*.

A good memoir of the Civil Rights struggle is Mary King's *Freedom Song* (New York, Morrow, 1987).

For a short and reasonable balanced view of the fight for equal rights, try *The Civil Rights Movement: Struggle and Resistance* by William T. Martin Riches (St Martin's Press, New York; Macmillan Press, London)

To look at the whole period, a real heavyweight study is *The Sixties* by British historian Arthur Marwick (Oxford University Press, 1998) – a dauntingly big book, but interestingly written.

Films

Sixties movies turn up all the time on television and are often worth watching.

Dr Strangelove: or How I Learned to Stop Worrying and Love the Bomb is a classic of 1960s satire, anti-war protest and nuclear paranoia.

What's New Pussycat?, a 1965 comedy, shows the '60s at their silliest and is packed with crazes of the time such as go-karts.

The Beatles' movies, especially *A Hard Day's Night*, are essential viewing for the decade.

If you want to understand what the 1960s did to attitudes, you could try comparing the 1960 John Wayne Western *The Alamo* with the 1969 *Butch Cassidy and the Sundance Kid*.

One of the biggest hits of the decade was *The Graduate* (1967). Starring a young Dustin Hoffman, and with a soundtrack by Simon and Garfunkel, it was the perfect 'generation gap' movie.

Bonnie and Clyde, also made in 1967, was essentially a 'youth revolt' movie, although set in the gangster era of the 1930s.

Films directly about the Hippie period include the disturbing road movie *Easy Rider* and *Alice's Restaurant*, both made in 1969.

There are two excellent documentary movies on pop festivals: the famous *Woodstock* and the less well-known *Gimme Shelter*, about a Rolling Stones concert at Altamont in 1969 that ended in violence.

Music

Much of 1960s music is familiar to everyone. Listening to Beatles or Beach Boys records in date order gives a run-through of changing '60s cultural styles.

You may not have heard early Bob Dylan songs such as 'A Hard Rain's Gonna Fall' or 'It's Alright Ma', a protest against the easy-listening tradition of pop music as much as against war and American society.

Miles Davis's 1960 album *Kind of Blue* is a reminder that modern jazz was, for many people, the in-sound of the start of the decade.

For a culture shock, it is worth listening to one of the popular '60s groups most people can't stand any longer – for example, the Incredible String Band or Leonard Cohen. Raid your parents' or grandparents' record collection. It is good to get a feel of the original albums in their 1960s record sleeves and to hear them on a turntable.

Art and architecture

Most modern art collections have paintings by '60s artists such as Warhol, Lichtenstein and Hockney, and works by Claes Oldenburg, Anthony Caro and other sculptors of the period.

Sixties architecture is only too visible in most cities, especially in the form of run-down council tower blocks.

Quotations

The quotations in this book are from the following sources:

Page 5: Jonathon Green, *Days in the Life*, Heinemann-Mandarin, 1988

Page 8: Ronald Fraser, *1968, A Student Generation in Revolt*, Chatto and Windus, 1988

Page 14: Marshall McLuhan, *The Gutenberg Galaxy*, 1968

Page 17: Rachel Carson, *The Silent Spring*, 1963

Page 18: *Harper's and Queen* magazine, May 1973

Page 25: Jonathon Green, *Days in the Life*, Heinemann-Mandarin, 1988

Page 27: Jonathon Green, *Days in the Life*, Heinemann-Mandarin, 1988

Page 28: Ian Chilvers, Harold Osborne, Dennis Farr, *The Oxford Dictionary of Art*, Oxford University Press, 1988

Page 31: Jonathon Green, *Days in the Life*, Heinemann-Mandarin, 1988

Page 34: Jack Nicklaus with Ken Bowden, *My Story*, Ebury Press, 1997

Page 37: Robert Andrews, *Dictionary of Contemporary Quotations*, Cassell, 1996

Page 41: as told to the author.

Index